TROODON

by Janet Riehecky
illustrated by Jim Conaway

THE CHILD'S WORLD

MANKATO, MN

*Grateful appreciation is expressed to
Bret S. Beall, Research Consultant,
Field Museum of Natural History, Chicago,
Illinois, who reviewed this book to
insure its accuracy.*

Library of Congress Cataloging in Publication Data

Riehecky, Janet, 1953-
   Troodon / by Janet Riehecky ; illustrated by Jim Conaway.
      p. cm. — (Dinosaur books)
   Summary: Presents facts and speculations about the physical
characteristics and behavior of this small, swift, carnivorous
dinosaur.
   ISBN 0-89565-636-1.
   1. Troodon—Juvenile literature.   [1. Troodon.   2. Dinosaurs.]
I. Conaway, James, 1944-   ill.   II. Title.   III. Series: Riehecky,
Janet, 1953-   Dinosaur books.
QE862.S3R539   1990
567.9'7—dc20   90-42925
                                                        CIP
                                                        AC

   3 4 5 6 7 8 9 10 11 12 R 98 97 96 95 94 93

TROODON

Though dinosaurs lived on the earth for millions and millions of years, scientists have been studying them for less than two hundred years.

At first, scientists had some strange
ideas about what the dinosaurs were like.
As they discovered more and more fossils,
though, they changed some of their ideas.

At first, scientists thought that all
dinosaurs were huge . . .

and that they could only move about
slowly and clumsily.

And scientists thought dinosaurs were stupid, barely smart enough to find something to eat . . .

and certainly not smart enough to work
together in a herd or take care of their
babies.

But now scientists know much more about dinosaurs. They have found many that are smaller than people. These and many of the larger ones could move quickly and gracefully. Scientists have also found that many dinosaurs were smart. Some lived and worked in herds or packs. Some took good care of their babies.

One dinosaur in particular changed a lot of old ideas. It was Troodon (TROH-OH-don). The Troodon was anything but a dim-witted, lumbering giant.

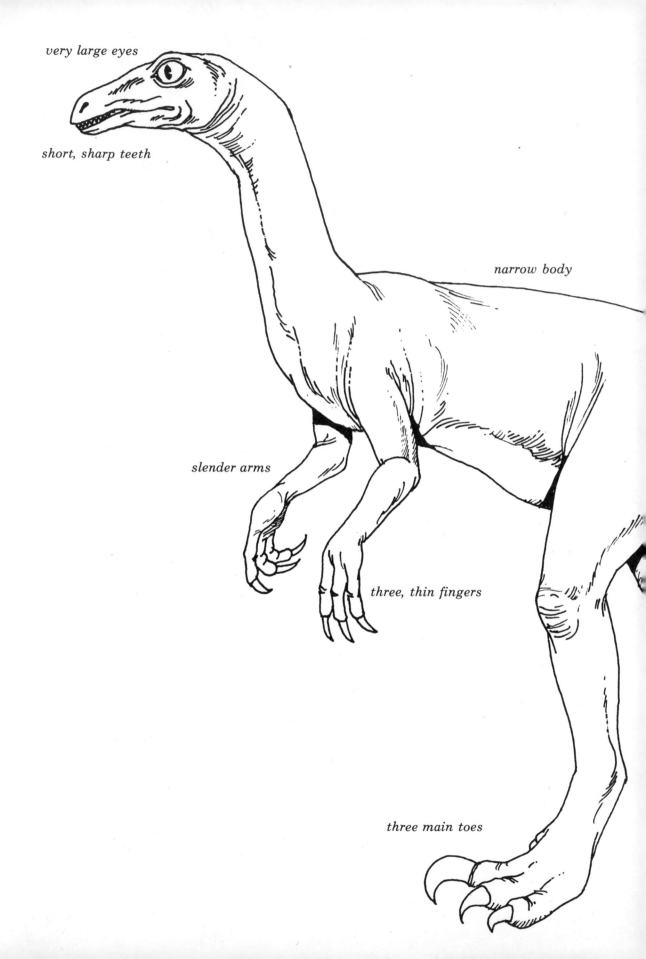

very large eyes

short, sharp teeth

narrow body

slender arms

three, thin fingers

three main toes

Troodon was only three or four feet tall and about six to eight feet long. It was certainly not a huge dinosaur. It wouldn't have even come up to the knee of a Brachiosaurus!

The Troodon may have been small, but it was fast. Troodon was a meat eater, and it could capture its prey by chasing it at great speeds—perhaps up to forty miles per hour! That's faster than any person can run.

long, stiff tail

short toe on side

second toe with large claw

Most scientists think the Troodon was a very good hunter. After all, it was a relative of the Tyrannosaurus. Its forward-looking eyes helped it tell how close its prey was. It also could hear very well and move quickly and gracefully. It led a very active life—quite different from the old picture of the slow, awkward monster.

When Troodon caught its prey, its claws made great weapons. On its second toe, it had a very long claw, which could slash up and down.

The Troodon also had many teeth. They were short teeth, but very sharp. In fact, the name Troodon means "wounding tooth."

The Troodon probably hunted many different kinds of animals. Its first choice for a tasty snack might have been a small plant-eating dinosaur, such as a baby duckbill.

But Troodon may have also liked to hunt at night when most reptiles sleep. Some scientists think that the reason it had such large eyes was to help it see well at night—which was bad news for the small mammals that thought they were safe in the dark.

There are some scientists that think the Troodon might have caught fish. The rough edges of a Troodon's teeth would have been good for holding onto something slippery that was trying its best to slide out.

Troodons may have hunted dinosaurs much larger than themselves. They may have hunted in packs and worked together to bring down an adult duckbill or some other large plant eater.

Picture a poor Maiasaura caught away
from its herd. A dozen Troodons dart after
it. They catch it easily and leap upon it,
slashing with their claws.

The Maiasaura stumbles and falls, bleeding from a dozen wounds. A quick bite in the throat finishes it off, and the Troodons have their meal.

Scientists think Troodons not only hunted in packs, but also lived together in packs. Troodons may have watched over their eggs, taken care of their babies, and protected their young dinosaurs against danger.

Scientists believe Troodons could do all
this because they had very large brains. In
fact, the Troodon was probably the
smartest of all the dinosaurs. Much of its
brain helped it to see and hear well, which

is what would have made it a good hunter.
But its brain was also big enough that
Troodons could have learned how to work
with others in a pack.

Was a Troodon as smart as a person? No. It probably wasn't even as smart as most of the animals alive today.

But two scientists once thought it would be fun to imagine how the Troodon might have changed if it had not become extinct and had become as smart as a person. They made a model of what they thought a modern Troodon would look like. It stood more upright than a real Troodon and had no tail. It was a sort of dino-human!

Other scientists laughed at the idea of a dino-human. They said that even if a dinosaur could have become as smart as a

person, it wouldn't have looked like a person. Troodon was a smart dinosaur, but it was still a dinosaur.

It's fun to think of what might have happened if the dinosaurs had not all died, but we can never really know. All that is left of them are bones, eggs, and footprints. This is all we have to give us our ideas about dinosaurs.

Dinosaur Fun

There is no such thing as a dino-human, but what if there were? Can you imagine discovering a live dino-human? Would it be friendly or dangerous? Would it be put in a zoo or taught to speak? Write a story about how you discovered a dino-human and the adventures that followed!